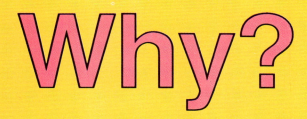

Why?

A DRAGON Question Book™

By Kathie Billingslea Smith
Illustrated by Robert S. Storms

A DRAGON BOOK

GRANADA

Why do things that go

When you jump up in the air, your body comes right back down.

Apples fall down from trees. Leaves fall down to the ground. All things that go up come back down to the ground. Something in the earth pulls them down. It is a special force called gravity.

up always come down?

Gravity works like a magnet to hold things close to the earth. You cannot see gravity, but it is always there, keeping houses, cars, tall buildings, lakes, rivers, all things — and you and me — close to the earth.

We are all special people born with our own special looks. We have a special colour hair, eyes, lips, and special colour skin. We cannot choose what colour we want to be. We are born with skin that is our own special colour. Children usually have the same kind of colouring that their parents and grandparents have.

different colours?

All people have a special colouring called melanin in their skin. Melanin gives colour to skins. People with a lot of melanin have dark-coloured skin. Light-skinned people do not have much melanin. If they go in the sun, they may get a bit more melanin in their skin — we say they have a suntan.

In some people, the melanin is not spread evenly over the skin, but forms small patches of colour. These little patches are called freckles!

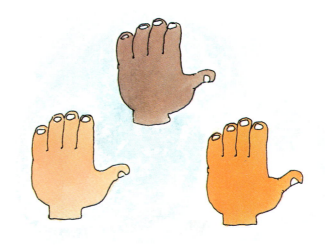

Why does the moon

The moon does not change its shape. It only looks like it does!

The moon is shaped like a ball. It is very dark, without any light of its own. But the sun nearby is very bright. The sun shines on the moon. Then the moon acts like a mirror and *reflects*, or bounces back, the light of the sun. What we call moonlight is really the sun's light bouncing off the moon.

Crescent moon

Full moon

Crescent moon

change its shape?

Sometimes we can see a lot of the moon. At other times, we can see only a little. This is because every 28 days the moon goes around the earth. We see a different part of the moon as it moves around us. When we see a *full moon*, the front side of the moon faces us. It looks like a big circle in the sky. But when we look at a *crescent moon*, we see only a tiny shining sliver of the whole moon. The rest of the moon is there, but it is hidden in darkness.

Why doesn't it hurt when

It doesn't hurt when you cut your nails or hair because nails and hair do not have any nerves in them. And nerves help us to feel pain.

cut my nails or hair?

When your foot touches the hot water in your bath (OUCH!), the nerves in your body carry a message of pain to your brain. Your brain "tells" you to quickly move your foot away from the hot water. This give-and-take happens faster than you can blink your eyes!

But when you cut your fingernails or toenails or get a haircut, it doesn't hurt at all. There are no nerves in your nails and hair to carry a message to your brain, so you can't feel any pain.

Why does furniture

It is late at night. You are lying in your bed trying to go to sleep. Then out of the stillness, you hear a noise.

CREAK!

It sounds very loud and a bit scary! But don't worry. There is a good reason for that noise.

During the day, the heat from the sun warms everything. At night, things cool down again. Your furniture gets a little bigger during the day when it is

make noises at night?

hot, and it shrinks at night when it is cooler. When this happens, a part of a chair or a table may suddenly slip a little. And . . . CREAK!

Houses and furniture make noises during the day, too. But we can hear the noises much more easily at night when it is quieter.

Why do leaves change

In spring and summer, most leaves are green. A special colouring called chlorophyll gives them their green colour.

When autumn comes, the leaves are ready to fall from the trees. Their stems begin to break away from the branches.

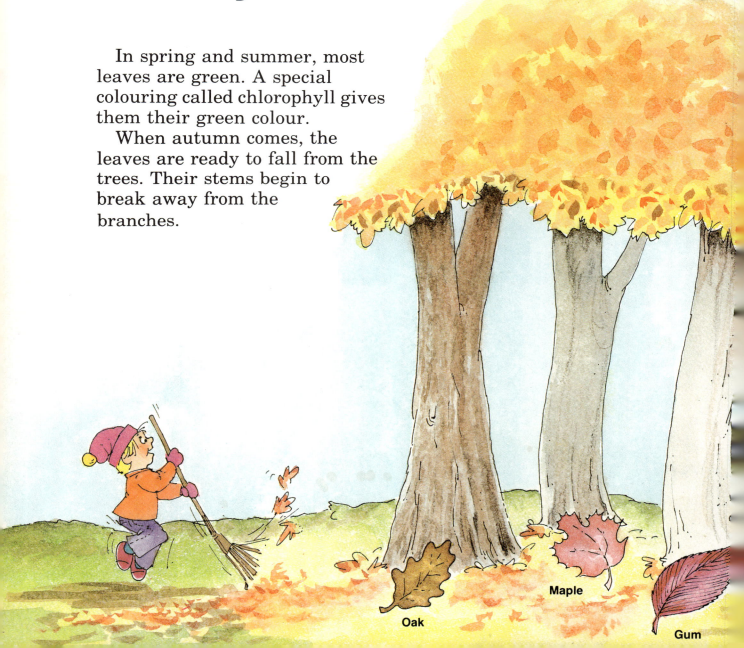

Oak

Maple

Gum

colours in autumn?

Then the leaves cannot get much of the water that comes up from the roots of the trees. Without water, the leaves' green colour fades away.

Then other special colours, or *pigments*, hidden in the leaves can be seen. Oak leaves change from green to brown. Leaves on a sweet gum tree turn a bright red colour. Maple leaves turn different shades of yellow or red.

Why is it cold in winter

The sun is a giant fiery star in the middle of the *solar system*, which is our family of planets. Our earth travels around the sun in a circle called an orbit. The earth is tipped at an angle as it speeds through space, and the sun heats the earth as it travels around the sun.

When the part of the earth where we live is tipped nearer to the sun, our weather gets hotter, because we are closer to the sun's hot rays. Then we have summer.

But when our part of the earth is tipped farther away from the sun and its warming rays, our weather gets colder. Then it is winter.

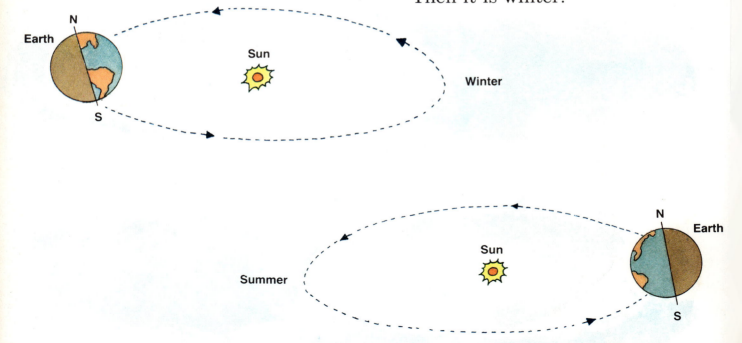

and hot in summer?

Hot and cold weather, summer and winter — all of these changes are caused by how far away we are from the sun.

Why do

Answer: "Buzz. Buzz."

bees buzz?

Wrong! Bees do not say "buzz buzz." In fact, bees do not say anything at all as far as we know. That buzzing sound is made by their wings, moving up and down very, very quickly. Honeybees move their wings back and forth more than 400 times each second or about 26,000 times a minute! Their wings move so quickly that we cannot hear each separate movement. Instead, we hear a buzzing sound!

Buzzzzzzzz! There goes another bee!

Most camels live in deserts where it is hot and dry and sandy. Food and water are hard to find. Camels need to carry supplies of food with them as they travel across the sand. These special supplies are in the humps on their backs! The humps are large lumps of fat that give the camels energy when food is far away. Other animals store fat in their bodies too. But only camels keep most of their fat in a hump.

...ave humps?

When camels have had plenty to eat and drink, their humps are big and firm. But when camels have not eaten for a long time, their humps shrink and become flabby. Sometimes the humps even flop over the camels' backs and hang down on their sides.

There are two main kinds of camels. Arabian camels have one hump. They live among the desert people of Africa and Asia. Bactrian camels have two humps. They can be found in Mongolia and other parts of Asia.

Why do some

Some people lose their hair when they get sick or when they do not eat enough.

But most people become bald because they have fathers or grandfathers who became bald, too. Baldness runs in families.

eople become bald?

Just like blue eyes or curly hair, baldness is something that parents can pass on to their children.

Usually baldness is passed through the mother's side of the family. So if your mother's father (your grandfather) is bald, chances are you could be bald one day too.

But if you are a girl, don't worry, since men are more likely to lose their hair than women are.

Great Grandpa Ed

Grandpa Edwin

Eddie Junior

Why does the tide

Waves roll on the beach all day long. Sometimes the sea rises up, and the waves creep farther and farther up the sand. This is called high tide or flood tide. The beach becomes smaller because much of it is covered by the sea.

Then the water level drops, and the waves do not come up as far on the beach. This is called a low tide or ebb tide. Shells and strange, wonderful pieces of driftwood from the sea are often left on the beach.

Tides are caused by the pull of the moon and the sun. As the moon goes around our earth, it acts like a magnet and pulls on the ocean waters. The sun pulls, too, but not as strongly because it is much farther away.

High and low tides happen twice a day.

High tide   **Low tide**

Why do zebras and tigers have stripes?

Zebras and tigers have brightly coloured stripes that make them easy to find at the zoo. But in the grasslands and jungles where these animals usually live, their stripes make them hard to see.

The zebras' black and white stripes hide them from hunters in Africa. The stripes look just like the shadows in the tall grasses where the zebras roam.

The tigers of Africa and Asia can hide easily with their stripes in grasses and bushes to surprise the animals they hunt.

The stripes these animals wear is called camouflage, which means they hide the animals from others. Animals that hide well can catch a good dinner, or they can miss being a dinner for someone else!